A HISTORY OF THE GARDEN

BOOKS BY KATHARINE COLES

The One Right Touch

The Measurable World

A History of the Garden

POEMS

A HISTORY OF THE GARDEN

KATHARINE COLES

UNIVERSITY OF NEVADA PRESS: RENO / LAS VEGAS

WESTERN LITERATURE SERIES

University of Nevada Press, Reno, Nevada 89557 USA
Copyright © 1997 by Katharine Coles
All rights reserved
Manufactured in the United States of America
Book design by Carrie Nelson House

Library of Congress Cataloging-in-Publication Data
Coles, Katharine.
A history of the garden : poems / Katharine Coles.
    p. cm. — (Western literature series)
    ISBN 0–87417–298–5 (pbk. : alk. paper)
  1. Gardens — Poetry. 2. Gardening — Poetry.
I. Title. II. Series.
PS3553.047455H57 1997   96–47670
811'.54 — dc21   CIP

The paper used in this book meets the requirements
of American National Standard for Information
Sciences—Permanence of Paper for Printed Library
Materials, ANSI Z39.48–1984. Binding materials were
selected for strength and durability.

First Printing
06 05 04 03 02 01 00 99 98 97   5 4 3 2 1

for Sherlie Baker, 1936–1993
and for Chris Johnson

CONTENTS

2: THE HISTORY OF THE BICYCLE

THE HISTORY OF THE GARDEN

1

FEAR OF FALLING

The night of my birth: the first time I was early,
a moon as full and hot as August
scraped the rooftops, a town exhausted

by labor, moral constancy,
and there was nothing—once you were emptied of me,
emptied of everything
subject to flushing, to medical starvation—

nothing in the town for you to eat.
The hospital kitchens were closed, shining and smug;
no all-night groceries, a decade before

twenty-four-hour convenience was conceived.
Over-promptness is a habit I keep.
Wondering, now, about finality—
my own and yours, which troubles you so little

and so late—I find you, late again,
living wildly, as if you were decades younger,
immortal and hungry. But I can't help

thinking of your late friend—late,
I mean, for good—falling back
through geologic time: sandstone
layered down through eons

by a sea now millennia dead.
At the canyon bottom, sand
filters soft as moonlight through the fingers
but gives no more than rock. It's simple:

he lost his grip. The biology
so difficult to learn — our brittleness,
how gravity reduces us to matter.

You might have been with him
but for coincidence, bad weather.
I don't mean to make light

of any of this — just to make bearable
details I invent for us to bear:
the moon's flight over my birth; your friend's

suspense; a canyon shaded
by red cliffs. I've invented your hunger,
but know it's true. After the service,

your friend's real body
undertook flames, the widow's journey
across the ocean, to a land hardened
by absence, too much green. Nothing

you can say. I believe
in your attention to hand- and footholds
less than in your desire for rock to carry you —
the soul of indifference — to the top,

where the surface was before
wind and water wore it down. Other parents

retire to Sun City, to swimming pools,
cultivated greens. They tend
their hearts. Your friend took

care too, or so you tell me, pressing
hands and feet to rock's surface,
testing each hold, even

the last. He trusted weight, his body's
resistance, to keep him here. All my life,

dreams have flown me
over the dizzy earth, my arms, my heart
lifting. Your friend's arms: did they fly
open when he knew? I remember your hands

stretching down to ease me over
a sheer edge, from terror into the view. It never stops.
In dream: how flight enters my body

and rises through it like laughter.
All those years, your bedroom door
opened for any sound. I don't look down. Now,

I invent your life and fix it here,
as if, without body and without right,
with only breath beneath it, a word could lift you.

for my parents, Salt Lake City, 1959–1992

DEATH VALLEY

After a painting by Maureen O'Hara Ure

More delicate than the historian's are the mapmaker's colors.
—Elizabeth Bishop

I. AT THE HOMELESS SHELTER SCHOOL

Leon's lucky pebble
is an entire desert
shaded red, ochre, violet—
all the colors brown
ever dreamed of flaming
under the sun's mirages:

that desert once held
the sea in its lap
and now holds a mere
hallucination of water,
bedazzled aridity
and a floor stark with salt's
impossible formations.

Anyone Leon shows
has to guess where it's from.
Now, the pebble sinks
into Leon's deep pocket.
Leon paints a red car,
sets it ablaze, sends it
over the cliff. At its window,
the requisite self-portrait,

the mouth's O of alarm.
"Where I'm going," he's written,
obediently, underneath.

He turns away from the camera,
will not say what he
and his father are hiding from.
The pebble has no weakness,
none it hasn't folded
tight in a gritty heart

beating so slowly
no one, in a lifetime,
detects that core of motion,
incomprehensible,
empty of any wind,
any stirring of sand or thirst,
any love or other violence
to send a flicker through it.

2. FAMILY VACATION I: DANTE'S VIEW
The Ford's blue wind
wavers on the air,
then falters, then winds down,
its engine puffing steam.
Dust settles around us,

but heat still blurs our vision,
the desert clarity.
Here, the terrors are only
fire, geology
the surface below expresses
in folds and rutting slabs.

We don't know how to read
the earth's explosive map.
Mother points and names

conglomerates and limestones,
igneous diorite
pressured over eons

then thrust up through the crust
to rest against the turtlebacks—
the very ground, tentative,
could open, take our bones
into the fossil layers,
the history of oceans,

of uplift and erosion.
We are children, tired,
restless under the heat
pressing us into the car seat,
but safe, somewhere to go

if we ever get out of here.
Below us, fields of salt
stretch under the sky
like glaciers, cool to the eye.
Father hasn't moved

his hands from the steering wheel.
Mother opens the car door
to a blast of arid wind.

3. FAMILY VACATION 2: LAST CHANCE RANGE
All the clichés: a grave,
railways drifted over—
not with snow, with sand.
Something built, abandoned
to what we can't imagine:
a desert valley so vast
we could cross for days

and not seem any closer
to the mountains on the horizon.
We look out of the windows.
Inches from our tires,
the road meets the view,
opens behind held breaths,

as if gates in our hearts,
creaking, have swung wide.
The thrust-fault's ancient rock
bucks, heaves the wagon.
Why would they bring us here,

into such precarious balance?
As if the rock will hold.
My father's face is set,
but behind his closed mouth
something flickers. Joy.
In the front seat, Mother's bandanna
glows red, combustible.

4. ARTIST'S PALETTE
   The painting is not the landscape,
   though we enter it, stroll under
   cliffs so bright we can't
   believe what we remember—
   such mineral brilliance
   couldn't, at last, be real.

   The poem is not the painting.
   The mind works the space
   between page and memory,
   a place recalled, acrylic

gold and red, complete
frigidity of salt.

We sit in a studio
high above our valley,
windows open to storm.
Clouds muscle over
snowed-in peaks of mountains
fifty-odd miles away—

a view domesticated
by habit, double-glazed glass.
We never tire of working
intimations of ice and sky
we delineate, try to enter.
We fail to enter our pasts,
much less other lives

less open to comfort than ours.
The poor will always be
with us, or without.
What we see is vast,
cool, immutable
rock and ages—not
the particular lives of the city,
its houses reduced beneath us
too small for habitation,

for their iced-over kitchen windows,
knives laid on the tables,
for the hands descending hard
or reaching up, open
to melt a space on the glass.

5. WINTER SOLSTICE
What we desire is more
distant, elemental.

From whatever threatens to move us,

we want to make some beauty
to cauterize the wound—
how Leon wound himself
around my legs, and held
so tight he bruised my thighs,

and then, as I was leaving,
told me to close my eyes
and dropped his charm in my palm—
it still held his body's heat—,

the pebble, to carry me home.
We return from the desert,

or from this afternoon's luncheon,
coffee, our voices and hands
fleshing out shapes on the air,
and let our house lights blaze

profligate on the twilight.
Again the dark descends
too early over houses,
freeway overpasses,
abandoned parking lots

where shelters made of cardboard
and scraps of carpeting
bend under the blizzard.
Our windows give us back

only our own reflections.
We couldn't see out if we tried,
not if we extinguished our lights,
cupped our hands to the glass—
unless we walked into the storm,

let its weight accumulate
and press our limbs to ice.
We wash the dust from our hair,
lie down on fresh sheets,
drive to the edge,

then over, into freefall,
family faces pressed
against the sandy windshield,
descending into the valley,
into prehistory,
as if this past, recharted,
could burn us clean of our lives.

THE WALK-THROUGH HEART

It is not in our stars, but in ourselves, dear Brutus.
—Shakespeare, *Julius Caesar*

I all but thought that the heart's movement had been understood by God alone.
—William Harvey, seventeenth-century physician

1. And so it is, whatever
maps illuminate

the body's circulation, meanders
of red and blue. Intention and the road

lead to destination,
or accident, the way

a cell, restless to follow
inevitable codes, multiplies,

breaks free, travels on the blood,
then sets root in lymph nodes, marrow,

brain. The seed blown
from lung or breast or bone. Nothing

we could have done. Driving
Soldier's Summit, at eight thousand feet

the canyon exploding
into sky, we thread rough country,

red cliffs curving into the eye—
but it won't suffice, this

displacement of grief onto landscape,
variable. Whole ranges lie

between us and that vast midwest,
insensible machines

    translating my husband's mother, breath
    and temperature, the heart's acoustic

throb. From her skull
the doctor lifts a shard curved like eggshell,

    lays it by on a towel, hefts his scalpel and leans
    over, to look inside.

2. In the museum, we had more
than metaphor—comic representation,

    mercy's human heart
    too literal, blown up

too much larger than life—less
credible than the jarred hearts of pigs

    pickled to brazen it out
    on the shelves of the high school lab.

Modeled to scale, it circulated
tourists: my husband and me

    and a troop of girl scouts, reaching
    to touch composite walls. So like

what we're made of: sculptural
papillary muscles, *cardae tendineae*

    branching, subterranean—
    a vessel to transport us

from the visceral to the aesthetic. That heart
was standardized, averaged, lit

like any other commercial cavern,
though each heart beats

measures individual
as each human face, and refuses

mortality. My husband named parts,
the sinoatrial node "self-exciting, kindling

the impulse, setting tempo."
When William Harvey held

that eel heart in his hand, it paced,
cold-blooded, toward an end,

as certain as Harvey's science,
his eyes, his touch, gave meaning.

3.   Concentration: we will
the blips on his mother's screen

to steady, carry her through,
while other machines perform

her body's labors. I have considered
the brain, when I thought of it,

as a tissue of ideas, the conscious self
working, abstracting the world, brutal

in its carnality. A poppy gracing its stem.
As if we were beyond mass,

cells alive with blood, with signals
sparking senses to move us.

As if we could leave it behind. This morning,
I peel off my gloves, drop them

to trace, right-handed, bindweed
roots through the soil. My fingers

    follow fiber, plumped
    rich with water. My left frontal lobe crackles,

receives sense. What fragments I miss,
out of sight and mind, will grow

    their own flowers—excited by rain, twining
    lilies, foxglove blowing

speckled, medical trumpets. Cure
or kill. Ancient Japanese

    called the heart *the realm of fire.* The brain
    we depend on has little

nerve. Her surgeon can turn it
inside-out: she won't feel a thing.

    It blossoms with impulse
    it refuses to contain.

4. The doctor talks about the other
brain, its failed memory. The body

    attacks itself. We compose
    what we must forget, minor

falterings, domesticated murmurs
we can't chart with machines, though my love is expert

    in such measuring. What grows
    behind his mother's brow and sternum

may pull loose from her cells, pull
away behind the blade, indifferent,

and that will be that. Chemicals, waves
of radiation. Kill

to cure. We count
percentages, years. Send flowers

she wakes to. The doctor tests with pins
what her right hand knows. More machines

cast light on buried shadows. Dreams,
however rooted, bound by blood

or mathematics, can't prepare us
for this: science illuminating

what it won't cure. What but science,
in its imaginings, could create a heart

scaled so like hers? Open
for us to stroll into, holding hands, naming

chambers more capacious
even than we desire—

more so than our own—
through which human voices sing.

for Chris Johnson, and for Sherlie Baker, 1936–1993

THE POEM YOU ASKED FOR

From your sickroom, with its lamps dimmed down
and curtains drawn against the outer light
you say you're leaving, against the green
lawn descending to trees that flowered for you
last spring, white clouds, your stray calico
mouthing her hunger and pawing at the door,
you ask me to find a poem to see you out.
I, who sleep all night to your son's rhythms,
curved around him, as the new moon bends
around her larger self, her fullness, in the dark
(the way your body now implies
just the shadow of its former shape) —
I sit and read for you, books open around me.
But I find in them only poems of this world,
of the blood-stirred bodies of bear and dog,
of trees beaten down by the midday sun.
Even the elegies walk their angry angels
down our human streets, through cities
dulled by use, the touch of human breath.
And though from your bed across the miles,
from your later time, you say you are ready,
how can we, not ready, broken-hearted
by rock and leaf and birdsong timed
sweet against its ending, believe you?
Until your husband lifts the phone to tell me
how he took the weight
of the body you can no more wholly bear,
and helped you to the window, your eyes blinking

away the sickbed dark: how you laid
your hand against the glass and looked through it,
through your reflected face, through the fall
flight of leaves, to the other side,
into that infinite world, like our bodies
so far away, composed of light.

for Sherlie Baker

VERA

I found her in the graveyard, on the hill,
the family plot—exactly where her mother
wanted not to end: among the other
four of her husband's wives. They're gathered all
at last around his knees, still patriarchal
even in their recent dustiness.
In this last commingling, the family flesh
is finally quiet, all old quarrels settled.
And Vera? Never married. She let pass
petitioners in turn. None quite suited.
All she wanted: to be left alone.
Pledged to solitude, did Vera find bliss?
Or only, well-matched, a jealous duty
she wrapped around, before she turned to bone?

THE HISTORY OF THE GARDEN

1. Where we are living our late youth, Vera
spun out her last decades of spinsterhood,
once the danger passed of anything more
than this for her. Each year the mountains
stayed frozen in through June then flamed, like now,
all summer long toward autumn, first wild fires,
then domestic, smudging the wind, leaves
fallen then fragmented to ash. Or
the other way around. Our neighbor says
these gardens were paradises in the wilderness,
so perfect in beauty you'd never know they thrived
on what was left to rot the year before.
Then, dim figures filtered down at twilight,
bending heads to bless the golden yarrow.

2. The Tuileries are dusty,
overlooked by angels
carved in the form of horses
turning their chiseled wings
over the open entry,
arched and edgy, as if
marble could climb the air.
Under them, children launch
boats across the fountain,
sails taking the wind,
making it visible.
All the gardens this autumn
pain us with their passing,
as we are pained by the passing
of buildings, the millennium.
Pigeons scuff the paths
onto which gesturing limbs
(and more private parts, reposed)
have fallen from the statues—
an ordinary woman, walking,
absorbed with her life's own weather,
brought short by extremity,
circles, glances around,
then heaves an arm to her shoulder,
carries it onto the Metro,
stands it, disarticulated,
in a corner in the hall,
smog-pocked thumb extended
for her husband to hang his hat on.

3. Our neighbor says if we want the angels to come
to life among our branches, or to drift
like shapely pollen among the lilies,
the domestic, still heavenly tomatoes
spilling seed where they fall, too ripe to stay,
we must succumb to a certain idea of order,
must take our tools to blossom and stem,
bind the heavy peonies upright,
stake the delphiniums, still so blue they dazzle,
even under our sky's interminable blue.
He's courting rain. Vera bent her head
one year under just such weather, a sun
that burnt her face, her garden, back to desert,
a ruin she took as a failure of tenderness.

4. At Giverny, looking down
from the bridge to the water,
we can't say which is the mirror.
Yesterday we swam
through the watery light
in the Orangerie basement
among lilies in bloom.
Today, the flowers are finished;
and didn't he, after all,
create the garden too? —
all the hand of courtship
cultivating perfection
and then painting, to fix it
in a certain light.
The lilies drift the border
between air and water,
between eye and canvas.
The fingers holding the brush —
everything slips through them;
everything, after all,
escapes. The bitter end.
If Monet once stood here
among sunlight's mirages
and lifted his hand, like this,
through air gone to frost,
what it brought back was an apple
like this one, past perfection.

5. When our neighbor bends his head toward
our not-so-careful chaos, our blowing weeds,
where Vera kept precise botanical time,
her blossoms pruned, her lawn fed, well-machined
against the chaste down-tick of her heart,
he only wants us to know about the chances
we're missing stubbornly, every day of summer.
We say *good evening* when the wind comes up,
but from the window we watch him into the dark:
he bends and pinches off dead heads
and spoons chemicals around his roots
and sniffs the air for what he cannot see
in what is, to us, still just the wind
bearing aloft the driest seeds of fall.

6. We find Père Lachaise
as the weather turns,
the breath of winter upon us.
At the gate, we buy a map
to guide us among the dead.
You're right: travel won't change us
in any material way—
tonight, an ache in the legs,
more from age than the walk
through this glum, humorous city,
and age is a novelty still,
just a trace, invisible
dust in our hair and clothes.
Here are too many buried
even for us to pay tribute,
at least on such a day,
the sky gathering seriousness,
and, outside these walls,
the cafés of the living
burning lights on the mist.
But just as we turn to leave
one grave pulls us short:
two men, life-sized in bronze
bedded down atop it—
not touching, but giving
the notion of an embrace—
naked, but modestly draped,
burned verdigris by the air.
Carved into their bed,
balloons, incongruous, tilt
empty baskets beneath them.

Dead, the inscription says,
together at the zenith—
rising into a view
that took them, exhausted them,
then carried them away.

7. In the morning, in the same decaying sweater,
he's pruning our old roses, the ones we've left
carefully to run astray. He never rests.
Shear blade hisses on smoothly sharpened blade.
He's already edged our grass the sidewalk's length
and brushed the dandelion leaves with poison.
Not yet forty, we think we've time to burn.
If he's learned anything, it's how to wait.
The dandelions, now, are green as ever.
Flowers fall under his shears. Familiarly,
he keeps courting his unruly angels
without distinction as to their beauty or virtue,
bickering with them under the fumble of bees
as they gather around the last sweet spoils.

DROUGHT YEAR

The orchard's on fire. This is literal—
turning, a new way. Not frost-snapped but dried
on the branch to tender kindling, fall leaves fly,
the air alight. The flame goes guttural
while he and I rush for water. All
for nothing: the bucket's rotted, the well gone dry,
a wilderness at our backs. Paradise
fallen under our care. He mutters, "Hell,"
metaphorical to the last. I'm put out.
The hair on my head rises to the flame;
my cheeks are burning. I know when I'm licked.
We'd left the trees untended, didn't doubt
we could recoup any time. Now we blame
the weather for the fruit that went unpicked.

NATURAL DISASTERS

1. A mother's lifelong rage. The slow burn
of a wire behind an old house wall, its paper
ornamental to the last, going

sepia before the fire
eats it out from behind.
                              No ignition:

in the end, at our old tinderbox,
no harm done. The firetruck bellied up,
sirenless, lights pulsing against the night,

and the fireman's industrial flashlight showed the source,
electricity turned to a slow smolder, smoke

we swam through.
                              In winter's dark, we warmed
our hands before the voluble
flicker of television, which brought disaster

safely into the designated room.
We bought it on purpose, the neighborhood's
oldest house. Walls dried to tinder. Walls at last so thin

one good jolt of earth (the fault
a block above us and poised to go, sometime
in the next millennium) would reduce them.

And then, of course, the mountain
crumbling down. We don't think

of the inevitable: empire fallen, citizens—
schooled in the way of a city
blazing like heaven's declension—

extinguished at once, our tidy block
reduced to rubble. On the tube,

families huddle in the cold,
their homes burned to ashes, or taken

by hostile forces, by dry rot, by the bank.
If we change the channel, famine burns

another continent's children to the bone.
We opened windows, let out the smoke.
It was as cold as our house would get all year,

though the weather was heavy, record-breaking.
Then we went to bed.

2.   Imagine this:
a man with a name requiring of him either
impossible dignity or the world's best sense of humor—

neither of which he's gained by fifty-six—
holds his hand to his heart, its charges

wired brilliantly awry, and falls
to his knees in a parking lot stitched with rain.

The janitor finds him. Too early—five A.M.—,
the hospital a block away sunk into winter half-light,

the ambulance drivers playing a game
of rummy. The emergency technician's hands
pumping down, electrical paddles to shock the muscle

back to the rhythms of work, of play. Too late.
Half an hour: entropy wins the day.

How much, in America, a white man's life is worth
(the Deep South; winter deeply green) —
more than anyone's on earth, and no more —

not even a life spent learning impulsiveness,
mapping tissues, the nervous skin

conducting the charge. He knew that machine.
Knew by heart his family's history.
Died, like everyone, surprised

by the fault ticking inside him. He paid it no mind;
had the words, but refused to name it.
All this, even his name, engraved

on the still electrified hearts of those left behind.
Over coffee, we shake the newspaper:

children, boulders, trucks plucked up, driven
inland by a tide we've ignored,

swelling so far out at sea, traveling,
we thought, to such desolate shores,

nobody paid attention
to the final turn toward our own beaches,
the building force.

3.   This couldn't be more personal,
or less so. The new year, 1993.
My mother will live for years,

her anger building like ice
she won't chip away. Her own mother
passed it on, and the world

collaborated—little endearments,
gestures, the weights of civilization

sticking like burrs around a heart
she will not turn to stone. I harden myself

to feel the ways I'm charmed.
In the yard, three feet of snow and counting:
icicles form on the eaves, blades

drawn toward us by their weight.
Another storm cauterizes our city.
All over the neighborhood, men scale

their houses' ice-glazed pitches, and start to shovel.
Their wives pace the walkways.
But roofs collapse in our best neighborhoods.

Drivers abandon their cars—suburban streets
lost to white, unpastoral meadows—

and forge on foot toward porchlights.
They will be lent the phone, then turned away.
From the whited-out mountains, a herd of elk

drifts toward the valley through a canyon
buried twenty feet deep in snow. Ghostly

in car headlights, the sensible elk
take the freeway the whole way down.
In the canyon's mouth, the wind

concentrates its rage on them.
Then they shoulder over snowbanks into our yards,
persistent as dream.

4.   Still there when we wake

to heavy skies, another storm barreling in.
They bare their teeth to the trunks

of cherry and dogwood. What we inherit,
too great a tenderness. I planted
those trees myself, but give them up

to watch the elk browsing,
lying in my yard's snow. On days like this

we may not feel luck churning
through us like blood. Look at that sky—

how history carries us here, a current
we're barely aware of. We don't resist

flying at the storm's eye.
This ring of peaks holds danger

back, makes the world peripheral.
But the elk are here. The cows, gravid,

sleep in our frozen lilies. And a fire burns
even under this winter, the dormant garden.
Above us, where the elk will turn

at first thaw, glaciers, traveling so slowly,
push before them mountains, reshaping the earth.

for T.P., 1936–1993

THE HISTORY OF THE BICYCLE

2

POEM FOR THE LAST DECADE

1. AFTER THE PARTY ENDED

We all came in from the streets,
left our confetti and bruised
rose petals for the sweeps.
They hauled away the rubble
to dumps, nostalgia shops
where chunks of wall, graffiti,
and the splinters of shop windows
nestle next to knucklebones
relinquished by martyrs and saints
of other centuries.
All of them forgeries.
No matter to faith. Still,
we had another decade
to weather. Nothing would end.

But let's start at the beginning—
or rather in medias res,
what in retrospect we call
the *Dark Ages,* because
science was out of fashion:
no physics but metaphysics,
alchemies of the soul.
All the flowers were wild,
and the castles chilly,
windows designed not
for panorama, but
for catapults, or household
items dropped with hot-oil
soup for the uninvited.

The unstudied classes,
in hovels trampled with mud,
warmed themselves over
the blazes of invasions

whose dates we memorized
while our century's late middle
wound down to another start.
Children, we were kept
in fortresses like theirs—
no windows tempting dreams,
on afternoons like this one,
of tulips burning down
before the storm's first wind.
And the women—pale,
with bad complexions (ages
before dermatology saved

our adolescent skins)—
each knelt before her lover,
or before God, for whom
when she opened, she really meant it.
I've read of the brides of kings,
but those brides of Christ were something—
flayed, impaled, beheaded,
their wounds ornaments
of transfiguring belief,
for which we feel nostalgia
we muster now, watching
atrocities edited
to fit the standard screen.
Surely, we could do something?

The wall falls, and then
off camera, just out of earshot,
a child begins to scream.

2. OLD HOUSES

But that was long ago.
We're sentimental
about things closer to home—
the view of the desert from
picture windows facing south
to capture spring's violent skies;
our buffed floors and woodwork
stripped of layers of paint;
the dust of past lives
whose tedium we fail to account
because the present drops
its veil over them
so only the luminous moments
shine through. We're enraptured
by these mute doorknobs
we scavenged one fall afternoon
in that dust-hazed Paris shop:
elaborated with swans
and stylized, feral boars.

From the desert to our deck—
where this afternoon
the cat, from the window's wrong side,
stalks a tarantula
stretching spiny legs
under a sun that's called her to rise,
though it is too early,

and in the sky clouds churn—
the distance is not so great.
Nor from countries across the ocean,
to satellites, in orbit,
to the antenna on the roof:
distress reduced to digits
we measure and transmit.
A matter of seconds, from
the driver's seat to the curb.
Consider your brother, lost

in this country's urban outdoors,
to the sky's most brutal whims.
In his brain opens
a dark flower, a hole
into which every particle
of light vanishes.
Finally, his name
will cross that threshold—
eventful, verging on blackness—
though we will keep seeing it

after it's lost to him.
The cat bats the glass
as if desire could melt it.
At least, as you say, it's spring.
Your brother would never return
to a city dulled like this one
with dust, the easy tricks
righteousness plays on the heart,
but you scan the faces of men
posed at freeway exits
and market parking lots.

What will they do for food?
You're looking for a sign,
looking less for him
than for any one familiar.

3. THE CHARM
In the cat's dream
desire becomes a bridge
that finally holds his weight.
He curls his paw and growls.
Dusk brushes the windows
with rain and leaves, blackness
crowding the panes, like a wood
worthy of any dark age,
any morality tale
in which the way back is lost.
At the piano, our voices
spiral a throaty staircase,
mount step-by-step a tower
that narrows until it opens
into shrill wind, a view
where heaven holds, still,
old charms, however tarnished.

Ordained by history
to doubt, to wait at the edge
of a desert scoured clean by weather,
we love its vaulted sky
for what science tells us it is—
static, dust and water—
in heavy books
only the faithful may translate.
Believe: there's nothing behind it

but more dust, light's refractions,
stars flying away
or collapsing into themselves.
In the first thousand years
Anno Domini, faith
knotted gentle ropes
around our necks, and led us.

Now, our fingers
rework the knots. Why not?
Theoretical strings of matter,
of heaven and earth, bind us
even more strangely
to divine spaces,
with particles so charmed,
so hypothetical we build
vast machines to speed them,
just so we can see

their traces, implications.
We've all the time in the world.
We knew we were impulsive:
the lightbulb flickers on
just like in cartoons.
But despite magazine photos—
computers illuminating
a hemisphere at a time
the weather inside our skulls—
we're easily bowled over
by conceptions of sky, of sun.
We raise ennui to an art
we work to make look easy.

Outside the darkened window
this desert's electrical storm,
however passionate,

is only the beginning.
We watch our fingers, reversed
in the steam-glazed bathroom mirror,
tying on the traditional
fin de siècle lace,
our hands soft as flowers
elaborating wrist and throat.
Bathed and perfumed, we engage
in immaculate courtships,
ignoring the violent flush,
the convulsions of our hearts,
though in the aftermath
we twitch and murmur, dreaming
out the code in our cells:
the cloud of the explosion,
the flower of heat rising
from the jugular. Blood on the tongue.

for Maureen, and for Fiona

HEGIRA

After a certain age, men never become really intimate, let their relations be
ever so close.   —Anthony Trollope, *The Bertrams*

So we joined up late—in the millennium,
in our youths, falling from us the moment
he leaned down and performed the ritual kiss,

the seal for all to see. The music started,
the piano unnerving the air. And then we drove,
though it was late already, toward Millennium—

a car packed full with champagne, honeymoon baskets,
off-white roses, their petals singed to brown,
he, his eye on the road, leaning over to kiss me—

through a night made so fierce by blizzard
we had to trust the storm's own furious flight
to carry us into the lateness, the millennial dark,

and to safety. That space we occupied
together had never seemed so small, so cold,
though I leaned into him, ready for his kiss,

under the heater's inadequate wind. We rose
into the mountains' white-out, as if scaling,
late at night, at the crisis of the millennium,

the walls of our city, set breathlessly high
in a desert silenced by that snow
leaning toward us, each flake a diagonal kiss

folding under the drifts. The city streets
turned in memory to a white, impassable maze.
It was too late. We were too far from Millennium—

and such a journey to start on, such a night
to fly from our lit house into abandon.
What had we to do with ritual's kiss? —

what right had we to expect our blood to spark
and fire us on our way? I touched his knee,
nostalgic already for him, the millennium,

but under my fingers sounded a single note—
terror, joy, the same low, tremulous tone
echoing through the late hour, through Millennium,
where he stopped the car and leaned to the sealing kiss.

PANTOUM IN WHICH TIME
EQUALS SPACE

Eugene would say, "Someone died. Time to redecorate."
Everything we owned was second-hand.
We needed to move. We were running out of space.
He cruised the Goodwill every weekend, collecting

anything he could find second-hand.
Suphlatus, angel of dust, was his guardian —
a sort of cosmic Goodwill queen, cruising, collecting
the dead like artifacts going to dust. First, strangers

made Suphlatus, angel of dust, their guardian.
Then he collected, one by one, our friends.
Dead as artifacts, they turned to dust, to strangers.
Joseph left a couch. Ted, a table. Odd chairs

collected one-by-one replaced our friends.
Hooked rugs, cookie jars shaped like dogs,
a couch left by Joseph, Ted's table, odd chairs.
When his last lover died, he told me, Eugene gave away

all the hooked rugs and cookie jars shaped like dogs
and checked into the Ritz, stripped to nothing.
His lover had died at last. Eugene gave way:
he threw off his clothes, his shoes, even his eyeglasses

and his checkbook; at the Ritz, he stripped to nothing
and scattered all he owned on the sidewalk below,
threw out his clothes, his shoes, even his eyeglasses.
Then he lay down on the king-sized bed and swallowed pills.

Some scattered. All he owned on the sidewalk below—
he planned not to need it. Doomed anyway, naked as death,
he lay down on the king-sized bed. He swallowed pills,
but not enough to do the trick. He was found in the stairwell.

He'd planned to need nothing, doomed anyway. Naked as death,
he let them take him. All he had left was grief.
It was not enough. Tricked out of the stairwell
where he'd carried the urn, full of his lover's ashes,

he let them take him. All he had left was grief.
When he got out, he burned up the asphalt west,
carrying the urn, full of his lover's ashes.
At the truck stop in Little America, the car burst into flame.

He got out, but the car burned down to asphalt.
He said, "Who can tell one ash from another?
At any little truck stop in America, flame is flame,
and ash is ash, no matter how it began."

Who can tell? One ash *is* much like another.
Eugene said of his lover, "So he was dense.
Ash is ash." No matter. He began
scooping a mason jar full of ash to label.

Later, Eugene said, "So my lover was dense,"
and he touched me. That was him: gallows humor all over.
A mason jar, scooped full and labeled "lover"
for Suphlatus to guard, dust of flesh and metal.

It always touched me, his gallows humor. All over.
Eugene was no Einstein. He's left me empty handed,
while Suphlatus guards his dust. He was flesh and mettle.

Now, his jar's packed in a living room full of boxes.

Eugene was no Einstein. He left me with time on my hands.
Someone died. Eugene would redecorate,
but everything's packed. The living room's full of boxes,
and I'm on the move. I've almost run out of space.

for Jack Droitcourt, and for Eugene Gudaitis, 1992

THE HISTORY OF THE BICYCLE

The world of our senses is comprehensible. The fact that it is comprehensible
is a miracle.   —Albert Einstein

I. ENGLISHER GARTEN

Ten minutes grace on the hour—we won't give up
a moment's balance, rented wheels
spinning us upright, with mathematical force

my husband explains. This wilderness, cultivated,
blurs by, no more familiar than that

abstracted world.
                            Historically, numbers describe
perfections. Our bodies remain

in motion, on this cool day their heat
dissipating on air. We thread

Sunday afternoon crowds, couples joined
at the elbows, mothers wheeling babies

past the Chinese tower, a Bavarian polka band,
the Japanese teahouse keeping

ceremonial time. I thumb my bell
to hear it, approaching the turnaround,

figuring our chances. On a bridge over
the River Eisbach, a man leans on his cane
and looks to the water, his white-haired wife

tilted half away—where were they fifty,
sixty years ago?
                            In high school math,

the teacher stepped halfway
to the wall, halfway again. In theory,

he'd never arrive.
                    Thirty-five minutes—time
half up. Not just our youths. History

rises in us, and faces that rise
from the water resolve into our own.

2. DACHAU
Climbing down from the train, we find
the bus-stop schedule—so little

said, and the directions in fine,
almost unreadable print, but the bus
will be on time.
                    Yesterday, as we toured

mad Ludwig II's Neuschwanstein, a storm,
as if on cue, blew through his Victorian

imitation medieval towers, slammed windows,
whistled—an authenticity

he couldn't have intended. The kitchens
spin with spits first dreamed

into motion by Leonardo, greased and fueled
by theories four hundred years old

when Ludwig assembled them here, still
high-tech for the day. Rain darkened

the murals of Parsifal, of Tristan and Isolde
drawn larger than life. In the theater
built for Wagner, no opera was performed

until 1933. Or anything else.
Mad Ludwig, before he could finish, was cast

into the lake by a lover, or drowned himself.
Nobody knows. The guide contrives a whisper.
A *male* lover, he says. Easier

to talk of a single death, love
glowing stagy over the distance. The plot
its own explanation.

But here,
as we get off the bus, the sun breaks through
and steams the gravel walks, lights up

the whitewashed museum and its washed-out stars,
black, pink, yellow;
an empty dorm
and bunks like bare cradles, too small

even for me. I can't explain how
to set foot in a place of wood and plaster,

ordinary, can be to enter a madness
machined into fine gears—how a needle

held in the flame keeps its line, though
its molecules accelerate, collide, brighten
into an instrument burning

under the skin, an experimental
pain. And we are looking—as always

too self-conscious—for sophistication,
some form we can carry through, without

turning away. In the end,
after documents in German, photographs
of medical tests and torture, empty ovens

undo us: sliding stretchers, the body's size,
roll by hand through arched doors, left open,

understated. This can't be understood,
though on the wall photos compose
limbs thinned to tinder, shapes we learn by heart

in black-and-white. At the sink, a sign cautions
workers to wash their hands. Standing here,
on this floor scrubbed by sun,

I no longer believe in my own distance—
just a man, his fingers held under the tap;

village housewives kneading, as I did last week,
the daily bread, understanding enough

to pass a crust when the guard turns his back.
Every atom composing us, its spinning nucleus,
could open into violence.

                              Walking back
on a greenly shaded path, with no sign
to help us on our way, we've never found more

places to rest—benches, a stream running
too quickly to return us to our reflections.

3. THE HISTORY OF BEAUTY
Schloss Nymphenburg

It's the palace my husband wants
to see, for its famous collection—not
the porcelain, nor carriages coronetted

in delirious ornament, nor fountains,
nor rare botanics, but this gallery
of lips and eyes. King Ludwig I was sane,

by comparison: he collected
women whose faces he framed, to fix
on the palace wall—the loveliest in Bavaria,

though my husband guesses (noting how
the beauty declines as nobility rises)
that some politics were exercised.

And who could have blamed the king, he says, if
the queens resembled their portraits? Amelia was no prize
in character either, perched in a gilded aerie

atop her hunting lodge, to shoot at game
servants on horseback drove toward her, then
retiring to nap in her mirrored room.

But, I say, what about Max's scurvy
eyes and invisible chin? The wig was only
fashion, a sign of the times, to be forgiven.

Peterskirche
If we were convertible, this would do it: flames
rising in golden chaos—no, not chaos:

explosive energy, perfectly composed—
to frame the altar. After all, the artist

knew God's perfect order, knew nothing
of the chaos we accommodate in our bodies,

charges we describe uncertainly,
in systems of equations, numbers so profligate

no human brain can solve them. So my husband
instructs machines to solve them for us. They count

even now, while he's on vacation,
the consequence of thought, or of passion,

the simulated stroke of heart or mind.
It's raining again, so we take our time

climbing the tower, to view a shroud of sky,
or peering at rococo choir stalls, into the dark

side chapels. Adam and Eve posed, flatly
medieval, against a garden without perspective—

her face has no sweetness to modern eyes;
it's double-chinned, as if, in paradise,

she was beautiful only by definition.
The first catastrophe: turning from the garden,

Adam opened his eyes on all that beauty
just there, manifestly beyond his reach.

Alte Pinakothek
Where did we see that Eve? In St. Peter's
or the museum? Under the café's smoke,

it runs together—the Gothic, the Baroque—
like in Italy, where we paced galleries
entirely walled with madonnas, or so it seemed:

every famous artist, and some just dead,
fleshing out the Annunciation. Degrees
of greatness, angles of passion. God's seed

falls to Mary's lap in stardust, an allegory
of the stuff we're made of, and a sign—

all that fancy gold leaf, expensive blue—
of the patron's worth. Even we,

nonbelievers, stand rapt before human faces
brushed with human joy, as before

extravagant Rubens, Breughel the Elder's half-
cynical exuberance, Hieronymus Bosch's
oddly scientific vision, bodies cast

into darkness, orbiting images bent
by forces we can't imagine, arriving like light
from the past. As by these faces around us,

also stardust, young, immeasurably laughing.
We ask each other which among them might be
most perfect, most according to type. We go

by bad American movies, our own faces'
inherited lines—wondering to what our genes,
in their inevitable turns, might commit us.

4. DEUTCHES MUSEUM
Strolling through the history of machines
he asks me, Why did they lose?

                              They seemed
to have it all: planes, subs, trains
you'd set this watch by, if it needed setting,

still oiled and ticking after three centuries,
still on time, still fixed
upon its golden chain. We're occupied

today by mechanics and device,
the evolution of vision, of lenses for viewing
the smallest objects, or the largest and farthest—

from beauty to precision. But it is
the bicycle gallery that holds my husband rapt:

two-wheeled hobby horses, carved and painted
with animal heads and bodies; velocipedes;

the Bavarian high-wheeler and English
ordinary; signs explaining

advantages over walking—some believed
such velocities would peel the face from its bone—

even an Italian tricycle, a gilded reproach
to all this efficiency.
                    The older the machine,

the better we understand it, as if at some point
nearing the present, our eyes, adjusted
to the past, refract the world, too complex

to be one thing. I say,
I have no idea. But this

telescope's brass collar, elaborated
with constellations, or this compass: they are machines
whose works are visible, not welded in code

on some inscrutable chip. A lighted panel,
secretive, blinks to instruct this model

reactor in committing acts of sunlight.
A simulation. The core exposed,
defused. A wall chart tells us: when

the focus fractures, its energy billows
fire beyond control, absolutely destructive;
then, slowing, it spends

its heat on air, loses all resolution,
drifts,
      leaving only ash
to settle, to work through the bone—still

beyond calculation, the inaudible
ticking away of half-lives, the long decay.

DARWIN'S ORCHIDS

Orchids were not made by an ideal engineer; they are jury-rigged from a limited
set of available components.   —Stephen Jay Gould

From so simple a beginning endless forms most beautiful and most wonderful
have been, and are being, evolved.   —Charles Darwin

And that was the end of innocence:
a shift from past tense, perfect,
presenting nostalgia's likeliest conjugations.
But it was a long time coming. The world
outside the garden blew eccentric weeds,
which flew botanical parachutes inside
the garden walls, then set to, and opened
flower by flower. Over time

the walls fell to dust, and all
that's been a paradise of boredom
becomes this dazzled wilderness,
new religion taking earth
by storm. What of it? What if even
the atom, under our cultivation, blossoms
unpredictably on its stalk of fire?
This butterfly does a perfect imitation

of an oak's dead leaf; this moth becomes
bark smudged black by human industry.
And this orchid in my window fashions
trapdoors for insects from its seductive petals.
And isn't all of it better, he might have thought,
buttoning his collar back in England, than anything
we might imagine? Better than Love herself

ascending a scalloped elevator from the waves,
one leg cocked? So the sun, no god after all

and too bright, keeps getting brighter. It burns
our eyes; because of our unmakings, burns
our cells into confusion, and is indifferent.
In the last century, Darwin paced
with his hands in his pockets, his eyes fixed
on the immutable island. And under his gaze

the world changes. A joke he takes well
to heart. Winding down another millennium,
we know more than we can comprehend. There is light,
and laboratory technicians peer through it, dismantling
into ever-smaller mysteries what makes us,
vanishing. Bodies illuminated, the flayed gene.
And this flower's divine coincidence of parts
turns toward my blazing window and opens wide.

THE ALL-PURPOSE ENDING

Our modern world embodies the clash between the consequences of
the recently discovered material order of the universe and the older, still
ongoing humanly created order.   —Heinz Pagels

I. THE FOURTH OF JULY

   Cherry bombs, sparklers—flame falls
   fantastic pinwheels at the Stadium of Fire;
   but the physicist's fire works

   another scale: pulsars, white dwarves,
   a baby universe spinning imaginary time
   from two black holes, dissolving,

   nobody ever sees. *The new material order:*
   numbers, some not real, tell us

   it is there.
                If I could keep a universe
   in mind, even Hawking's baby, hypothetical

   (less the great wall's galaxies, spanning
   half a billion light years), while light
   falls over my window seat, ordinary—

   but I seldom think, lifting my face
   to the sun, that it's another star,
   and a minor one.
                   A week ago, heaven fell

   so near, we seemed, on mountain's edge,
   to drive through a cosmic architecture,

   but sank, instead, into the sleeping valley,
   taken by gravity. The yellow moon

cruised the peaks, a fin
slicing granite waves, invisible teeth at work.

One woman unable to follow

the simplest map, the other ready to guess
where any road might end, arbitrary, let
whimsy thread them through summer

homes rich enough to use
geology, or cosmology, as decor: windows

instead of paintings, fixing, in daylight,
mountains, at night this island
universe, fast behind glass walls.

2. LAWS OF CONSERVATION
    We'd descended from such art, soft
    backlighting, melting flesh on the tooth,
    service so transparent it didn't matter

we hadn't earned it,
                                    and the planet
kept rotation, kept ticking out equations,

working the laws of Newton—his old chair
held by Hawking, born three hundred years
to the day after Galileo died.

                                    It goes on:

Einstein born the year Maxwell died,
and Maxwell in Newton's last year, and so on—

what my husband calls *conservation*
of physicists, as if the mind of God
accommodates only so much competition.

As long as he was able, Hawking murmured
to a student, an oracle, translating.
Now, Hawking clicks with his right hand,

scanning a digital menu, assembling
voice. Deus
ex machina. In the end, we are taken

by his charm.
                This morning, I set down
my book, the laws

I embody, conserving energy. Outside,
students dig our garden: the word *hooter*

arrives on a wave: — *oo* — ,
the voice crests,
                    breaks
over the *T,* then swishes

to a stop, *braggade*
caught, like desire, in the throat. Breast

reduction rid a girl of the speaker,
a truer lightening, it seems from where I sit,

than surgery will usually accomplish.
Tonight, the moon will cruise, predatory,
almost full, shifting to its rule

this little lake, my body, pulling eyes
up. It never fails to move.

3. THE ALL-PURPOSE ENDING
A final gesture
sends us into starlight, asks it to take us
in, to comfort, in spite of the cold

spaces it travels—the mind of God reduced,
an act of closure. My words

reshape memory, define our distance
from it, though I imagine our end: us
with our eyes lifted

to the numinous sky.
                              That mountain,
when I was a child, was wilderness,

chaos of blue lupine, asters
the owners call weeds. Those houses,

in their log-cabin style, were built
to carry us back, to days
science updates, makes simple: electric

disposals, trash compactors, pasta
makers, as if we can have our nostalgia

and eat it too. We do. And machines
dispatch blips from planets, discover
six moons we call *new*, as if our gaze

opened the galaxy to them. Once, we were
the center. Or at least those men,
multiplying abstractions, gravitational

masses full, halved, quartered
by reflected light. The mind of God

upon them, they survived, by turns, the heat
of constant thought. We inhabit
lives as if we've made them, words

to fashion a world. Science says
God created a language to work
all matters; imagined pure numbers

the physicist sets loose, to order
a universe. Did Hawking's baby
exist before Hawking conceived it

on the page?
                And these words—
I close my eyes and turn them. Worn
grubby by human use, freighted

with implication, they spin out in my mind
our spiral through the dark, all that talk

chaotic. Like the path
of the least particle science imagines,
ours won't reduce to equation, won't yield

to shortcut, so becomes its own
most accurate description.

for Cynthia Macdonald, author of a talk by the same title,
after hearing Stephen Hawking

ELEGY FOR A DOG LARGER THAN LIFE

The true atheist is he whose hands are cauterized by holy things.
—Francis Bacon

Blind, he swayed his head at our voices,
side-to-side, like a ponderous bull—

Christmas, three-thirty, a morning struck by ice.
We held him through the seizure, the coughed-up blood—
our arms' embraces not enough,

it seemed, in that cold dawn to keep him with us
through the failure and surge of his brain's electricity
which seared through his flesh to our palms as we steadied him—,

then carried his not-quite-dead weight downstairs
on a makeshift litter. A hundred-forty pounds
felt like childweight, though he stood the whole way down,

his feet tearing through the old wool of the blankets.
It should have been funny. So much of his life

had been devoted to comedy, the slapstick gesture
grown large, overstated. We shepherded him

straying into a night lit by blizzard,
only our voices leading him to our will.

He followed as if by instinct, as if by love.
No other cars on the street, no guiding lights

but our own, reflecting back at us on the storm
as we slowed for the traffic signals, then ran through.
Not a night for proportion. We arrived,

lifted him out, left the car door open.
Still lost, he followed us in through double glass doors,
past the darkened tree, the cards strung up

in the waiting room, down a hallway, toward the light.
Spat more blood. Never stopped believing

we'd lead him right. In the examining room
he paced between us, laid his head on my lap,

his body pinning us, holding us in orbit.
Whatever we'd believed in — science, art,
the curve of space, what is visible only

once the eye is trained to know it's there —
had prepared us after all for his faltering breath
no better than myth, than incomprehensible heaven

opening wide its comforts. Not at all.
This was certain: his big body stuttering down.
He wanted to be with us, wherever we were,

but when the doctor came to lead him away,
we walked him as far as the doorway, then came back alone

to the room where we waited, blood on a yellow floor.
We needed a miracle, to dim the clinical lights.
What we had: a mirror, paper towels,

to wipe his blood from the tiles. The dead hour.
Outside, the blizzard kept up its intemperate raging,
and we pressed our palms flat against the wall —

as if we could feel the storm through drywall and brick —
for all that laughter that had lumbered out of reach,
down a hall barely lit for just such emergencies.

THE PHYSICS OF FLIGHT

1. Some nights, our bodies become
all we want. Some days
they're spaces we arrange
our lives' matter around,
the way I fiddled
the folds of Grandmother's dress—

silk and lace, a past
I put on, to marry—
around a body prepared
with unaccustomed perfumes,
as if such art could make it,
for one night, unfamiliar,
before the familiarity
we'd contracted set in for life.
Dire, conventional promises

no mortal can comprehend,
no one whose blood beats
into lips they press together
the moment speech fails.

No wonder our hands were shaking.
Grandmother was looking on—
a visibly unwinding
example of entropy,
testily herself—
from under her nylon wig.

2. How can we imagine
any end? In that dress,
my grandmother drove through the night,
her new husband beside her.
Still drunk, still in love,
they arrived at dawn in Chicago,
their train already blowing
its soot on the winter air:

headed for the coast.
That marriage would never last,
though its image arrives
like starlight out of the past.
Now, you can barely see it:
the stain of champagne that spread
through the white silk on her bosom,
the visible sign of a joy
she refuses, now, to confess.
Then, her foot pressed the gas

all the way, into a future
already past for years
the night we lifted our glasses.
Still, our friends, dizzy with hope,
passed us all night, aglow,
from embrace to safe embrace
before they released us to darkness,
to each other and winter's first snow.

3. We can't bear to think,
this long night of flight
far above an ocean
deeper than we can imagine,
of the air: it bites
a chilly darkness around us.
And dawn will come,
since we're flying east into sunrise,
hours before we're ready.

We're no nearer the stars,
though we're miles from earth.
Everything you've told me
about the physics of flight,
about lift and stress,
impossibility—

I hold your hand in my lap,
keep myself from asking
how far we would fall
before we could fall no faster.
Now, it's you afraid,
you who know too much
about machines, disaster.

On the way back over,
this short night will give
to interminable afternoon.
I have been thinking, while
you watch the in-flight movie,
how marrying you was like walking
blind over the edge,

opening into an air
that somehow held
against the laws of nature.
Why has it taken years
before I would write for you?
As if my words would make
too thin a shell to bear
our flight into the world.

4. So that night, we danced
a little too wildly, as if
to push at the edge of the dream
that had seemed to hold us for weeks,
the heart's machine working
away at the mind's questions,
and answering, *faith, faith,*
electrical, impulsive.

Then I caught a heel in the lace
hem of my grandmother's gown,
and that was it. Its fabric
couldn't hold my body
against the pressures of time.
No woman will wear it again.

Late that night, at home,
I boxed its hand-shirred tatters,
slid it under the bed.
As silk and lace transmuted
into a dust we breathed,
you laid yourself beside me —
your hands, for once, were cold,
though I was the one afraid—
the same, but changed
by a few words, said
so even I could answer.

for Chris

ACKNOWLEDGMENTS

Poems in this book have been published or accepted for publication in the following magazines: "The Physics of Flight" and "Darwin's Orchids" in *American Literary Review*; "Vera" in *Connections*; "Drought Year" in *The New Republic* vol. 197, no. 4, issue 3784 (July 27, 1987); "Natural Disasters" in *The Paris Review* vol. 36, no. 132, Fall 1994; "Pantoum in Which Time Equals Space" in *The Paris Review* vol. 37, no. 135, Summer 1995; "Elegy for a Dog Larger Than Life" in *Poetry*; "Death Valley" in *Quarterly West*; "The History of the Garden," "The Poem You Asked For," and "The All-Purpose Ending" in *Tailwinds*; "The Walk-Through Heart" and "Hegira" in *Weber Studies*; and "The History of the Bicycle" in *Western Humanities Review.*

"Death Valley" was reprinted in *Tumble Words: Writers Reading the West* (Reno: University of Nevada Press, 1995) and in *What There Is: The Crossroads Anthology* (Salt Lake City: The Crossroads Urban Center, 1996); "Poem for the Last Decade" first appeared in *The Sacred Place* (Salt Lake City: University of Utah Press, 1996) and will be reprinted, along with "Natural Disasters," in *The Millennium 6 Anthology* (Washington, DC: The Millennium 6 Project, forthcoming).

A History of the Garden was written in collaboration with visual artist Maureen O'Hara Ure. *Natural Disasters,* the resulting installation, showed at the Finch Lane Gallery in Salt Lake City. Maureen's direct and indirect contributions to these poems, and the importance of her friendship, are too great to measure.

I would like to thank the organizations whose grants supported the writing of these poems: the National Endowment for the Arts, the Salt Lake City Arts Council, and especially the Utah Arts Council, whose Publication Prize has been only the last and greatest of many generous gifts, financial and otherwise, that have made the writing and publication of these poems possible.

Kenneth Brewer, Richard Howard, David Lee, Cynthia Macdonald, and Mark Strand have my thanks and love for their invaluable advice and steady support, as does Trudy McMurrin, whose generosity, humor, and sharp eye make her the best possible editor.